FRESH A.I.R.

Brent Earl Aldom

ISBN 979-8-89309-334-6 (Paperback)
ISBN 979-8-89309-335-3 (Digital)

Covenant Books
11661 Hwy 707
Murrells Inlet, SC 29576
www.covenantbooks.com

Contents

Preface

> I'm starting with the man in the mirror
> I'm asking him to change his ways
> And no message could have been any clearer
> If you want to make the world a better place
> Take a look at yourself, and then make a change.
>
> —Siedah Garrett

In July 2018, as my son was deeply entrenched in his church service mission and teaching English to middle-school-aged students in the Mongolian capital of Ulaanbaatar, *Time Magazine* printed an article describing the horrific pollution smothering the city. The thick, opaque smog blanketed the horizon, and it was the first time I truly realized the sacrifice my son was making. Most major metropolitan areas deal with the devastating effects of pollution all the time, but this was somehow different. This touched home. This was my son! Why was he wearing a mask over his face? He was literally suffocating and in dire need of fresh air.

But it wasn't just the smog that was making it difficult for my son to breathe. He struggled with the fact that the Mongolian culture tolerated a certain amount of abuse against women. As he struggled with the cultural differences, I reassured him that he was making a positive difference in the world just by being himself.

And there it was; the proverbial lightbulb went off in my head. Not the old, soft-white incandescent bulb from the Bugs Bunny cartoons of the 1950s, but a bright, modern, daylight LED bulb. I was preaching change to my son, but in reality, I was not practicing my own advice. In order to change the world, we need to focus on the one person in whom we have control: ourselves. I wallowed in doubt and misery as I watched the world deteriorate before my very eyes, but I was doing nothing to change it.

In January 2019, I made the obligatory New Year's resolution. I was going to use my writing to spread a message of inner strength and encourage people to change the world by changing themselves. If every person only focused on changing themselves, then one by one, we could change the world. And while it seemed like a ridiculous thought at the time, I knew that changing ourselves was much easier than forcing change on others.

Unfortunately, I allowed procrastination to set in. For all of 2019, I did nothing with my inspiration. I dabbled here and there, but never truly dove right in. I embraced impostor syndrome as I convinced myself my message wasn't worth spreading. My New Year's resolution vanished as quickly as the inspiration appeared.

Then it happened! Nearly eighteen months after ignoring my inspiration to send a message of hope and change, the world as we knew it simply stopped breathing, literally and figuratively. This time, it wasn't a visible, tangible smog like my son experienced in Mongolia. It was an invisible culprit that hit unexpectedly and created worldwide panic. The world was now in the deadly grasp of a respiratory pandemic, and people were once again struggling to breathe. This was serious; the world was being placed in quarantine.

As this pandemic spread unabated, the panic increased exponentially. While true heroes like first responders, doctors, and nurses placed themselves on the frontline putting their own lives at risk, the media incessantly reported on only the negative aspects of this global tragedy. They looked for scapegoats to blame.

Soon, the worst side of humanity reared its ugly head. Medical misinformation ran rampant on social media. News corporations intentionally used photos from foreign countries to stoke the flames of panic. It seemed as if everyone was seeking to place blame or find a scapegoat. Fights broke out as people hoarded hand soap, disinfecting wipes, baby wipes, and toilet paper. Retailers couldn't keep up with demand for these products, so their workers became targets of verbal hostility and abuse. In a time of crisis, instead of coming together, we were torn apart. Society was literally and figuratively suffocating due to a microscopic virus!

But what if we had been forewarned of the dangers caused by embracing our inner dark side of humanity? Regardless of one's religious affiliation or lack thereof, the words from the biblical prophet Isaiah seem eerily accusatory of our current situation.

"Woe unto them that call evil good, and good evil; that put darkness for light, and light for darkness; that put bitter for sweet, and sweet for bitter!" (Isaiah 5:20).

Could it be possible that our current disrespectful behavior toward our fellow human beings is merely the symptom of rejecting Isaiah's admonition for decades? If so, what might some of the examples of "calling evil good and good evil" look like? The mere identification of socially acceptable evils instantly creates controversy and ensures personal attacks on those who dare speak out against these bandwagons. Under the politically correct guises of tolerance, acceptance, and freedom, society now endorses evil as good.

No further example of the slow degradation of society is needed than to look at twenty-first-century role models. Over the past fifty years, society has replaced police, military, teachers, parents, and religious leaders as role models with morally bankrupt athletes, Hollywood actors and actresses, and politicians. While neither every athlete, actor, actress, or politician is the embodiment of the evil Isaiah warned us about, nor every police officer, soldier, teacher, or parent is the personification of purity and goodness, generally speaking, society has replaced positive role models with those who embody greed, entitlement, and corruption. The quiet, respectable greatness of Cal Ripken Jr. and Michael Landon has been replaced by outlandish, bombastic reality television stars whose actions are often questionable at best. Obviously, we have walked, or perhaps ran, off course.

Whenever I hike in the woods and feel like I have lost my way, I stop, take a deep breath, and look at my compass. Society, too, can get back on track if we all decide to stop, take a deep breath, and look at our compass. While no one is suggesting that there has ever been a perfect society, it can be argued that the twenty-first-century version has completely lost its way. One thing about being lost in the city is that we are still enveloped by pollution and smog. It's difficult to see or think clearly. But when we are lost in the woods, when we step back in time before progress polluted nature, we have the opportunity to see clearly and breathe Fresh A.I.R.

In 2018, I was metaphorically enlightened to start a new path, but it took a medical pandemic nearly two years later for this epiphany to motivate me enough to encourage the world to change, one person at a time. But for me to motivate others, I had to start with the most difficult test subject: me! I needed to step out from the smog and breathe some Fresh A.I.R.

What Is Fresh A.I.R.?

Fresh A.I.R. is a conscious choice, a change in mentality, and a paradigm shift where we consciously and intentionally embrace the reality that all our decisions and actions can be tied specifically to the intersection of three simple character traits: accountability, integrity, and respect.

All life choices and decisions will affect, either positively or negatively, at least one of these three traits. To change ourselves, we must first define these traits. Definitions must come first, as they are the foundations upon which change is built. Without a proper foundation, everything we build will eventually collapse. From there, we need to examine ourselves honestly and without prejudice. Finally, we must act. If we want the world to positively change, we must focus on the one person we can actually change: ourselves.

Step 1: Definitions

So what is *accountability* exactly? *Merriam-Webster* defines *accountability* as a "willingness to accept responsibility or to account for one's actions." But Fresh A.I.R. takes this definition one step further and requires us to be accountable not just for our actions but also for our thoughts and decisions as well. The reasons for including thoughts and decisions in the definition are simple: First, our thoughts dictate our actions. Second, our decisions may result in *inaction*, so sometimes what we don't do is as important as our overt actions. If we choose not to act, we are still accountable for the results because we made the conscious decision not to act. Personal accountability is becoming a fading character trait. Its declination can be attributed to many factors including extreme political correctness, disreputable politicians, television, movies, loosening morality, and the inability to accept our individual imperfect humanity. Perhaps we should consider the admonishment of Mahatma Gandhi when he stated, "It is wrong and immoral to seek to escape the consequences of one's acts."

C. S. Lewis described *integrity* as doing the right thing when no one is watching. *Merriam-Webster* defines *integrity* as a "firm adherence to a code of especially moral or artistic value." Integrity is becoming more elusive in modern society, so this trait is often one of the more difficult, perspective-altering character changes we face. What do we do with that money we found on the ground? It's not ours, but how often do we just pocket it? "Finders, keepers," right? This decay in personal integrity is not surprising; we are bombarded by stories in the media or television that endorse dishonesty. Children are often confused by the mixed messages they receive from social media, television, and sadly, even within their own homes. Moreover, as integrity fades, so, too, does respect.

Albert Einstein once explained *respect* in this manner: "I speak to everyone in the same way, whether he is the garbage man or the president of the university." This profound statement accurately illustrates *Merriam-Webster's* definition "to consider worthy of high regard." As we seek to change our perspective of the world, we must first change our perspective of others. Respect is often the cornerstone of relationship building. If our thoughts, decisions, or actions intentionally come at the expense of others, we will always live in a hostile environment. Much like the smog in Ulaanbaatar, tension can suffocate our interactions. When we are disrespectful to others, we guarantee that our own learning, happiness, and interpersonal relationships will never bloom.

Step 2: The Mirror

After defining these traits, it was time for me to look in that proverbial mirror, and I didn't like what I saw. While accountability, integrity, and respect were always important to me, I realized that I wasn't always embracing them as tightly as I thought. Years of being bombarded with negativity had worn me down. I became cynical and maybe even mean-spirited at times, especially when the very traits and values I held most dear were under attack. I realized that I was suffocating from the negativity; I was the one who needed a breath of Fresh A.I.R. It was time to start with the man in the mirror!

One of the difficulties with voicing a plea for individual change is the personal scrutiny by cynics and critics who wish to deflect the focus from the pure message to the flaws of the messenger. Whether intentionally or not, when someone points out our weaknesses, we immediately become defensive. We then point out the faults in others (or in the person suggesting we change) to justify that we simply "aren't that bad." Comparison is one of the most dangerous attributes humans have adopted because it is often used to rationalize our weaknesses. If we appear just a small step higher than someone else, we convince ourselves that we do not need to change. We stagnate in a fixed mindset and cannot become better human beings. Our thoughts become our own limiter: "It's just who I am, so deal with it!"

Unfortunately, even if we consider changing for the better, society has been groomed to believe that if the messengers are not perfect, their messages are equally flawed. Consider how difficult it is for people to give credit where credit is due if an idea originates from a person outside of their political, religious, or societal spectrum. How many messages have we quickly discarded simply because we did not approve of the messenger?

If we are honest, we will acknowledge that this happens more frequently than we care to admit. Personally, this was one of the most difficult realizations for me to overcome. But once I focused on the *message*, I was able to gain a broader perspective. Suddenly, the message became more important than the messenger. Identifying, analyzing, and considering messages allowed me to focus on what I may learn rather than merely focusing on how to tear down the messenger. There was liberation in this realization!

For three years, I refused to spread Fresh A.I.R., partly because I believed I had to be perfect to convey my message. I finally grasped the concept that my message was pure, so I didn't have to be perfect. Besides, even if I were perfect, my message most likely would offend a certain portion of the population. But that doesn't mean my message should not be heard. The seeds of change had been planted inside me, and they were now taking root!

"Positive" Roots

Since its birth, the United States has been touted as the land of opportunity. For nearly 250 years, people have flocked from around the globe for the chance to enjoy all the blessings freedom has to offer. In the seventeenth and eighteenth centuries, humble individuals and families braved the treacherous journey across the Atlantic Ocean, sacrificing everything they had back home. When they reached their destination, their hearts were filled with thanksgiving. After all, the opportunity they longed for was now a reality. Despite being destitute, many of these immigrants viewed their circumstances as the first step toward achieving their dreams. Their optimism drove them to succeed. This optimism sparked the idea of the American dream!

Admittedly, this country has had its dark moments. We must not ignore this darkness, but rather, we must use those moments as motivation to never stop improving. Our history is messy. From racial inequality to Native American cultural annihilation, our country has always been flawed. But these lessons have taught us how to become better. We cannot change our country's history no more than we can change our individual past. Sometimes, it is in our darkest moments that we learn the most.

Yet despite all its past and current mistakes, the United States is still a beacon of optimism and hope. Recent history, however, suggests that citizens have lost their optimism for their country, which often translates to a loss of hope and confidence in themselves. The question "What if?" that inspired so many of the country's great inventors has been replaced by a pessimistic "Why try?"

But if we remember the sacrifices of those who built this country, if we focus on the lessons learned instead of looking for scapegoats to blame, we can fully embrace the *message* of this country as espoused in our Declaration of Independence: "We hold these truths to be self-evident, that all men are created equal, that they are endowed by their Creator with certain unalienable Rights, that among these are Life, Liberty and the pursuit of Happiness." Their message was pure, even if the messengers were imperfect.

Pessimistic Weeds

Although the United States was built with strong, optimistic roots, even the strongest trees eventually will be choked when weeds overrun the landscape. The noxious weed of pessimism is now suffocating the country. Fueled by a never-ending attack on the values of accountability, integrity, and respect, cynicism and pessimism have replaced hope and optimism as core values. Gone are the days when teachers, police, clergy, and our brave soldiers in uniform were respected. Instead, these true heroes are now portrayed as the enemy while criminals, corrupt politicians, and Hollywood actors and actresses cast themselves as role models while constantly posting to Twitter, Facebook, Snapchat, and other social media platforms.

The rise of social media has been a double-edged sword. On the one hand, social media allows friends and family the opportunity to follow the lives of their loved ones more closely. Grandparents can instantly see photos of their grandchildren playing in the autumn leaves. Parents can post family photos as their daughters pose with Elsa on their trip to Disneyland. Friends can connect instantly from thousands of miles away, fostering friendships that previously may have dissolved due to distance. For many, social media has been a blessing; for others, however, it has been a curse, like crabgrass in their lawn or Japanese beetles tearing through the leaves of their maple trees.

As with most technological advances, social media is often used as a weapon to spread evil instead of a tool for the promotion of harmony. The twenty-first-century version of "keeping up with the Joneses" has taken a dangerous turn as people compare their lives with the Utopian false narratives that their Facebook friends post.

Why are they always so happy while I am miserable? How come they are always on vacation when I can't even afford to take a day off? Why are they always driving new cars while I am stuck driving my piece of junk?

As we humans increase our reliance on digital technology, we are witnessing, or perhaps *causing*, the decline of accountability, integrity, and respect. Instead of spreading positivity, social media is now being used to spread hatred and negativity. The 2022 School Crime Supplement (National Center for Education Statistics and Bureau of Justice) found higher percentages of public schools in 2019–20 than in 2009–10 reported problems with student cyberbullying (16 vs. 8 percent) at least once a week (Véronique Irwin[*]).

Cyberbullying is on the rise while political propaganda, half-truths, and lies are spread freely and without recourse.

Worse still, social media addiction is tearing apart families as husbands, wives, and children waste hours every day posting comments to social media, hours that could be spent enjoying quality time together playing games or even simply talking with each other. As the Academic Support coordinator at my local community college, I watched students struggle daily to verbally communicate or to even make eye contact. Social media addiction is so powerful that it is now more common to see people on dates spending much of their time on their phones texting and posting to social media than communicating with the person they are supposed to be spending time with. No wonder there is such a lack of respect in this world!

The Garden

When we look out across our earthly garden, does it seem like the chore of removing weeds is hopeless and overwhelming? After all, it does appear that the weeds of negativity and pessimism have a stranglehold on society. Nothing is more depressing than watching

---

[*] Véronique Irwin. "Report on Indicators of School Crime and Safety: 2022 and Indicator 2: Incidence of Victimization at School and Away from School," *Bureau of Justice Statistics* (n.d.), https://bjs.ojp.gov/library/publications/report-indicators-school-crime-and-safety-2022-and-indicator-2-incidence.

the nightly news or visiting online news outlets. Murder. Rape. Child abuse. Wars. Rumors of wars. Corrupt, power-hungry politicians. It's nearly impossible to find positive, uplifting stories.

In order to save our positive roots from suffocation, we must act. And we must act now! The longer we wait, the stronger the weeds get, and the harder they are to remove. We must weed out pessimism and negativity. It is time to strengthen our own roots and take back our fertile soil. It's time to spray some Roundup on the weeds of social media and news outlets.

While it may seem impossible for one person to change the world, we need to remove this negative, fixed mindset. This book isn't about changing the world. It's about changing ourselves. And we all have the power to change ourselves! When one person changes, friends and coworkers notice. Family members notice. Everyone around them notices. Soon, society's entire outlook on the world will change. And this is how we can eliminate the weeds of negativity. One person at a time. One mindset at a time.

Everyone seems to be inhaling the smog that has settled on the valley of our divided society. It's time to escape that smog. It's time to take a trip into the mountains, high above the polluted mindsets. It's time to breathe some Fresh A.I.R.!

Before we actually breathe Fresh A.I.R., we need to acknowledge our personal weaknesses and embrace certain beliefs which will guide our actions moving forward. This may be uncomfortable at times, and certain statements in this book may ruffle some feathers. Because our thoughts ultimately control our decisions, it is necessary to change our mindsets before we act. This change may include having to accept some harsh realities about ourselves and embrace a little tough love as we change the reflections in our mirrors. In the end, Fresh A.I.R. will weed out negativity and fertilize our brains with positive thoughts and improve our relationships.

TENET 1
Don't Procrastinate!

You may delay, but time will not.

—Benjamin Franklin

You might be asking, "Why is this the number 1 tenet?" Simple. Procrastination is the largest obstacle to all success. We have all, at one time or another, fallen victim to the destructive consequences of waiting until the last minute to accomplish a task. How many of us waited until the night before to study for a final exam or to write that essay and then barter with our teachers for an extension on the assignment due date? Or perhaps we are always "fashionably late" to social events? How many of us have felt those awkward, accusatory stares when we walked in late for church as we stared at the floor to avoid eye contact and rush to find a seat?

Yeah, I know; we've heard a million times how we shouldn't procrastinate. When it comes time to make personal changes, it's easy for us to just put it off for a day or two. But the biggest test of our commitment is our willingness to take *immediate* action. One thing I've learned while hiking in Glacier National Park is that if I don't make that hike today, the unpredictable weather or the rogue grizzly will stop me tomorrow.

My personal road of spreading Fresh A.I.R. was plagued with potholes. Every time I gained some momentum, I drove right into the pothole of distraction. Whether the distraction was digital in nature (social media, streaming videos, online news websites, etc.) or more tangible (family, work, life responsibilities, etc.), instead of avoiding the pothole, I drove right into it, breaking my axle and stopping me dead in my tracks. Repairing the axle took time, and by the time the axle was replaced, it seemed my battery was dead, and I could not get started again.

Unfortunately, distraction eventually leads to procrastination, and procrastination is a weed that doesn't require deep roots in order to spread. The 3:00 p.m., five-minute pothole of checking emails or social media quickly turns into two hours of wasted time. Before we know it, the afternoon is wasted. Now it's dinner time, and our five-minute break just extended another hour. It's now 6:00 p.m., and now it's time to settle down for the evening. But don't worry, we'll get right back to it tomorrow!

Unfortunately, once procrastination spreads, it suffocates everything, including our accountability, integrity, and respect.

Procrastination and Accountability

When we procrastinate, we give ourselves an excuse to not be held accountable. We claim we "don't have the time" to accomplish important tasks. But often, the reality is that we had enough time, but we procrastinated. We try to convince ourselves that it's not our fault, but until we take responsibility for our actions, or lack thereof, nothing will change. We will continue to make excuses instead of being accountable.

Unfortunately, there is no single catalyst, no individual weed, responsible for the decline of personal accountability. Instead, numerous societal noxious weeds have sprung forth, many sprouting alluring, beautiful flowers to confuse us. These ideologies are often initially altruistic. However, just like weeds, when these ideologies are left unattended and allowed to sprout wildly and out of control, they become destructive.

For example, the idea of a "participation trophy" was initially well intended. In fact, the idea is nearly a century old. In its rawest sense, it sounds quaint. Anyone who participates will be awarded a memento. After all, as we get older, these mementos will spark joyous memories. Much like grading with gold stars and smiley faces, the initial intent was to encourage our best efforts. But the idea of the participation trophy was unbridled, much like the use of gold stars and smiley faces. Eventually, their original intent was smothered by a layer of noxious weeds disguised as beautiful wildflowers.

As the twentieth century entered its last decade, the idea of the participation trophy sprouted offshoots. Again, these offshoots were initially well intended, but they grew without restraint and began to overwhelm the trait of personal accountability. Suddenly, participation trophies led to the idea that everyone should make the team, regardless of individual skills, motivation, and/or work ethic. Under the guise of inclusion and acceptance, this ideology disintegrates the very fibers of personal accountability. The effects of this mentality are devastating. We place a cocoon around our children to protect them from feeling the pain of disappointment and failure. But what happens when these children grow up?

Whether we choose to admit it or not, the stereotype of "entitled" placed on millennials is understandable if not expected. After all, since they have never experienced failure as a youth no matter what their skill or effort, why would they expect adult life to be any different?

Candidate: "What do you mean I didn't get the job?"
Employer: "Well, we decided to go with another candidate with more
    education, experience, and a proven track record of success."
Candidate: "But…but…I applied!"

While this example seems overly simplistic, it is more prevalent in our culture than we may choose to believe. I've helped hundreds of job applicants revise their resumes, and I am amazed at how many applicants "tell" about their skills instead of showing. And nearly everyone claims to have "a strong work ethic." When applicants ask me why they did not get their interview, I simply point out that they merely told the employer the same thing every other applicant does. I explain that they need to start *showing* how they are accountable in the workplace.

Procrastination and Integrity

Perhaps we have never connected the dots before, but the more we procrastinate, the more we damage our personal integrity. How many deadlines have we missed at work not because we did not have enough time to complete our task but simply because we procrastinated?

Think about it; procrastination does not necessarily mean being idle. On the contrary, we often put off tasks simply because we do not want to do them, so we find other activities instead. We are putting off our primary task for one that is less obnoxious in our minds. When the boss asks why it didn't get done, we claim we were "too busy," which, in a sense, actually is true. We embrace the excuse because we are not actually lying. We *were* too busy to finish by the deadline…too busy doing anything else but the task we were assigned.

As a nontraditional college student, I listened every semester to the frantic pleas of my classmates as they begged the instructor for more time or leniency when they did not meet an assignment deadline. Yet these were the same students who bragged every Monday about their partying escapades over the weekend while I spent my weekend juggling homework, employment, and being a husband to my wife and a father to three active sons.

I struggled to lend an empathetic ear; in fact, I was appalled by their lack of integrity. I could not understand how they could ask the instructor for more time or leniency when they just spent the past thirty minutes bragging about the amount of alcohol they consumed or the hours they wasted on the latest video game!

Unfortunately, it wasn't until years later that I realized I was looking back at myself at their age. The frustration with my classmates' lack of integrity was a manifestation of my own failures at their age. I began to accept the fact that when I was their age, I was guilty of using similar integrity-destroying procrastination tactics my classmates were using now. Sometimes when we look in the mirror, we don't like what we see, and I realized I was repulsed by my own reflection.

Procrastination and Respect

When we stop to think about it, procrastination is one of the most disrespectful things we can do to ourselves and to others. When we procrastinate, we limit our own potential as we stockpile our responsibilities. Simple tasks become insurmountable obstacles simply because we choose to wait. Our responsibilities never disappear simply because we put them off to a later time. In fact, procrastination makes our future lives more difficult.

Consider our garden analogy; when is it easiest to weed the garden? Is it when the weeds are few or when our garden is overrun? By procrastinating, we turn weeding into a seemingly impossible chore. Eventually, we give up, and our flowers or vegetables succumb. When our friends ask, we simply state that we didn't have time or that we could not keep up with the weeds. Regrettably, the uncomfortable truth is that had we not procrastinated, the flowers and vegetables would have prospered, and our harvest would have been plentiful. All our initial hard work preparing and planting the garden was futile. Why would we allow all our hard work to be wasted? Moreover, why would we disrespect ourselves in this manner?

The ripple effects of procrastination reach far beyond our individual spheres of influence. When we procrastinate, we often adversely affect others who are depending on our actions to move forward. Our procrastination stagnates others, and few things could be more disrespectful than limiting the growth and accomplishments of others. Worse still, consider how procrastination affects those closest to us. Have we allowed procrastination to get in the way of quality time with the ones we love most? Have we ever told a child we were too busy to spend time with them and never considered the reason we did not have time was because we procrastinated?

Sadly, by procrastinating, we do not give ourselves or the ones we love the respect they deserve. We do not share our most precious commodity, our time, because we choose to stockpile our responsibilities. We are often left emptily proclaiming "I love you. We'll spend more time later, I promise!" Unfortunately, "later" often never comes because we continue to procrastinate. These empty promises show neither love nor respect, yet we rarely consider procrastination as disrespectful.

Tenet 1 Challenge

Create a schedule for the next thirty days. List all tasks and goals you must complete. Give each goal a specific starting date and date of completion. Check off each goal/task as you complete it. At the end of the month, review your schedule. How well did you complete your tasks as scheduled? Note any tasks where you procrastinated or delayed starting. Did procrastinating prevent you from completing other tasks? If so, identify these incomplete tasks. Finally, document any factors that contributed to your procrastination. Write down any suggestions you can use to prevent these factors from hindering you in the future.

TENET 2
Offense Can Only Be Taken; It Is Never Given

Take no offense. That which offends you only weakens you.

—Wayne Dyer

Of all the Fresh A.I.R. tenets, the suggestion that people take no offense may be the most controversial and emotionally charged. For some, this chapter may cause them to stop reading any further. But for those who choose to embrace positive change, the reasoning behind this change in mentality is undeniable. The less offended we allow ourselves to be, the less contentious our interactions with others will be. It truly is that simple.

As I grew up, I remember being repeatedly admonished whenever I whined about someone calling me a name I didn't like. I cannot count the number of times I was serenaded with "Sticks and stones may break your bones, but names will never hurt you!" At the time, this adage annoyed me, and as a child, I didn't appreciate the fact that no one cared that my feelings were hurt by someone's mean words. But a funny thing happened: I grew up. I realized that words only have power over me when I *allow* them to have power.

For the past four decades, the destructive nature of *extreme* political correctness has weakened us as individuals. Initially, the ideology of political correctness was closely connected to respect. Instead of treating people rudely and making demeaning comments, political correctness offered a positive alternative to society's unbridled disrespectful nature afforded by our First Amendment right to free speech.

Somewhere along the way, political correctness lost its way. Just as people took freedom of speech to its extreme, supporters of the political correctness movement did the same. Over time, *everything* we said became offensive. The old "sticks and stones" adage drastically changed to "Sticks and stones may break my bones, but name-calling is a million-dollar lawsuit!" People are now afraid to say anything at all; and this is dangerous for the individual, the community, and our nation.

Undeniably, the original intent of political correctness still makes sense today. As humans, we seem to have lost our sense of respect. However, the extremeness with which we have embraced political correctness, it can be argued, is more destructive than the disrespect it was meant to eliminate. Too many people are looking to be offended. Harmless statements are suddenly analyzed and taken out of context to create offense. This is the reason for the invention of emojis. Nowadays, people are so quick to find offense that they literally seek it out even in the most benign, benevolent situations.

I remember as a young teenager I attended an event with a guest speaker who spoke of the evils associated with our musical choices. Targets of his venom were the usual suspects of the time: AC/DC, Van Halen, Motley Crue, KISS. Of course, we teenagers already heard this before; rock music was Satan's tool to capture our souls, and we were all on a downward spiral to fire and brimstone. Blah, blah, blah…I remember losing my interest and the speaker's voice sounded like Charlie Brown's teacher in the old cartoons. But then he crossed the line…his desire to take his message to the *extreme* led him to claim that John Denver was Satan's servant. I lost it. In a crowded auditorium, I raised my hand. He stopped his talk and asked, "Yes, young man. Do you have a question?"

I stood up and raised my voice so all in the auditorium could hear, "John Denver is satanic? Really?"

"Yes," he smugly replied. "John Denver sings about getting high and—"

I cut him off. "We aren't the satanic ones, you are!" I aggressively asserted. "Anyone who finds Satan in John Denver must be *looking for Satan*." The audience erupted in thunderous approval, and I was immediately escorted out of the auditorium for my disrespect.

Ironically, his message—his words—offended me, and I responded like most teenagers do with a disrespectful retort. It wasn't until years later when I fully understood that I had *allowed* that person to offend me. His message wasn't any different than the hundreds of others I had heard before, yet I took exception to it unlike any other time previously.

So let's embrace a new approach and adopt a new tenet: "Offense can only be taken, it is never given." In other words, let's consider what happens when we embrace the mentality that no matter the verbal grievance against us, it is still in our power to choose to be offended or not. How many times have we said to someone, "No offense"? The natural reply is always, "None *taken*."

By embracing this second tenet and consciously limiting how often we allow others to offend us, our lives will be less contentious. Our proverbial relationship harvest will be abundant. If we embrace the adage, "I won't take anyone personally unless they are fogging up my glasses," our lives automatically become more optimistic. And we won't be wasting time and energy seeking out the hidden offense in others' statements.

Offense and Accountability

When we are easily offended, we create scapegoats and built-in excuse makers. Someone hurts our feelings, so we take offense and retaliate. We use offense to justify our poor decisions; after all, we simply react to what someone else said or did to us.

Retaliation is an easy way to avoid being held accountable for our actions. After all, as long as we didn't start it, we have every right to defend ourselves, right? Well, yes and no. And the line in the sand is physicality.

If someone threatens us with bodily harm, it is perfectly acceptable to defend ourselves. In fact, if we don't defend ourselves from physical harm, we become targets and victims. Having raised three sons, my wife and I quickly learned that bullying was prevalent in our public schools. So we raised our sons to never instigate a physical altercation. If we found out they started the fight, they would be in more trouble at home than at school. But if a schoolmate threatened them physically, our sons had our blessings to defend themselves.

Those were the clear lines in the sand: Our sons could not justify their actions if they instigated the altercation, and they were expected to defend themselves if they were physically threatened. The threat of physical harm was the only instance we allowed them to take offense. Any verbal insults or name-calling were not justification to be offended.

However, this is not an excuse to encourage physically solving problems. On the contrary, most physical altercations start with words, with name-calling, with insults, and yes, even threats of violence. When someone's words hurt our feelings or are threatening, we quickly take offense.

But what if we didn't take offense at any words, whether verbal or written. Think about it; people have become victims of *words*. The only way words can hurt is if we give them the power to do so. How much cyberbullying can occur if we ignore words or shut off social media? How much power do words truly have if we simply ignore them? This includes all manner of culturally offensive words: personal insults, ethnic and racial slurs, political ideologies, religious beliefs, etc. Reacting aggressively to these words is what gives them power.

By giving words this much power, we weaken our personal accountability. Instead of being offended by every word that someone says or writes, imagine how much more peaceful life would be when someone used "offensive" words and we laughed them off or simply ignored them.

Offense and Integrity

Remember that speaker who claimed that John Denver was satanic? I allowed myself to be quickly offended, and in doing so, not only did I get removed from the auditorium, but I also allowed my personal integrity to be removed as well. Looking back to that fateful day, by taking offense, I did not firmly adhere to my own personal code of moral value. I was only then realizing the importance of having a voice. The idea of free speech was merely a novelty I studied superficially in history classes, but I hadn't yet embraced its power.

Just a few years later, however, as a senior in high school, I was introduced to the concepts of censorship and bandwagons, and apparently, I was on the wrong side of these ideologies. My high school history teacher and her student-teacher mentee were staunch and vocal supporters of President John F. Kennedy, and they made the class aware of their biases. They also expressed their disdain for the current president at the time, Ronald Reagan. This was not exactly shocking; after all, I did attend school in Kennedy's home state of Massachusetts. JFK's pictures and quotes covered the classroom walls, and rarely a day went by without an allusion to our thirty-fifth president, regardless of the day's topic. Most of the class quickly jumped on her bandwagon. Unfortunately, I was one of the few who did not embrace her perspective.

For most of my senior year, my friend Paul and I were the targets of insults, not just from our classmates but from the teachers as well. In one of the most gratifying moments of my high school years, Paul and I were intentionally placed on a team in our history class to debate two of our senior class's more recognized scholars on the pros and cons of the industrial revolution. The class laughed as the teams were set; it was obvious that Paul and I were headed to slaughter. As the debate unfolded, however, something strange happened. We were winning the debate. Not just winning; we were completely dismantling the other team. As the class observed in stunned disbelief, the other classmates and even our teachers intervened on their behalf. When we continued our dominance, the debate was quickly shut down.

Looking back, at this moment I embraced the importance of free speech as part of my moral code. I didn't like how Paul and I were silenced simply because our thoughts contradicted the bandwagon. Ironically, it wasn't until years later that I truthfully analyzed my response to the speaker who questioned my choice in music. I was guilty of trying to silence his message. It took nearly a decade to admit that my actions in the auditorium that day were hypocritical. How could I claim to have any integrity when my actions suggested otherwise?

Ask yourself this question: "How many friends have unfriended me on social media simply because of my words, political views, or comments?"

When we are quick to take offense, we accept more than hurt feelings. The ripple effects of taking offense may damage our personal integrity which, in turn, damages our ability to build or sustain stable relationships. When we do not practice what we preach, we make it impossible for anyone to truly trust us. And if we are easily offended, even our closest friends will wonder if the next comment they make on social media will irreparably destroy years or even decades of friendship.

Offense and Respect

In that moment, I viewed my "performance" in the auditorium as my life's crowning achievement to that point. The student had upstaged the teacher. The applause and cheers validated my actions that day. As I was being removed to the delight of my peers, I gloated. For weeks, all I talked about with my classmates was how "I showed him." But what had I "shown him," really? That I was a pompous, disrespectful jerk?

The more easily we become offended, the more likely we completely lose our ability to respect the other person from whom we took offense. Look how I treated the speaker simply because he spoke words to which I took offense. At that moment, not only was I being disrespectful, but I was totally incapable of showing respect. My feelings were hurt, and instead of seeking to understand his message, I chose to be impolite and rude. While it temporarily satisfied me knowing I had gotten even with the speaker, I look back now and realize this wasn't my crowning achievement. It was one of the lowest points in my life. I had convinced myself that my actions were justified. But were they? According to the paradigm shift associated with

Tenet 2, the answer is a resounding "No!" Once we accept that words are not justification for taking offense, we can clearly see my response in the auditorium was wrong.

Tenet 2 Challenge

For thirty days, track how many times you were offended by someone's words. Whether a political difference or a simple difference of opinion, what sparked the offense? Keep a diary or journal of all the times you took offense to someone's words, written or verbal, and write down how you responded. Then describe how you can avoid being offended by these words in the future.

The following is an example:

Words to which you took offense	What sparked the offense	How you responded	How you can avoid taking offense next time
"Someone called me…"	Political argument about…	"You are a…"	

TENET 3
"No" Is a Normal Part of Life

To be without some of the things you want is
an indispensable part of happiness.

—Bertrand Russell

One of the most frustrating societal changes I have personally experienced is the inability for people, especially parents, to use the word "no" and then enforce the decision. Nearly every time I go to a store, I see parents tell their children "no" when they ask for a toy or for candy only to watch as the kid pitches a fit until the parent finally succumbs and buys them something. What message does this send to the young child? Obviously, the child learns that in order to get what they want, all they need to do is make a scene.

But parents aren't the only culprits reinforcing the belief that saying "no" really means "yes" if we complain long enough (and loud enough). Many school administrators have become more like politicians than educators and do not have the backbone to stand behind their decisions. All it takes is for an angry parent to storm into the office and threaten a lawsuit, and their demands will be met, even when the parent or the student was in the wrong.

But we can't simply lay the blame on a few bad parents or school administrators. Society itself must shoulder the blame here. By adopting extreme political correctness as its guiding light, society encourages and fertilizes these noxious behaviors. Somehow, it is now considered evil to explain to a child they may not have the talent necessary to make the team. Everyone must win. Everyone deserves a trophy just for participating. Again, what lesson does this teach the child?

Under the guise of acceptance, instead of saying, "No, you did not make the team" and encouraging the child to work harder and try again, we impose the damaging, false doctrine that just because we try, we will automatically be successful. Moreover, we weaken these children's ability to handle adversity in the future. No wonder people have catastrophic mental breakdowns when they don't get the job they apply for or when their politician loses an election. By removing the word "no" from their vocabulary, they simply assume life will continue without obstacles or setbacks. We complain that the younger generations have a sense of entitlement. Well, why shouldn't they? Every person they have known has refused to use the word "no" around them. If the younger generations feel entitled, society must bear this burden.

No and Accountability

Though comprised of only two letters, the word "no" is one of the most important words in the English language. When used properly, it has the immense power to develop personal accountability.

In order for children to learn the importance of taking responsibility for their actions, they must first understand that certain behaviors are not acceptable. Children must learn that if they are told "no," there will be consequences should they choose to defy the directive. But telling a child "no" does not mean that we remove their free will. Sometimes, in order to learn, we need to let the consequences be the teacher.

Years ago, one of our sons was repeatedly told not to go near the stove while it was hot. It seemed like this became a daily game; he would put his hand near the burner and wait for mom or dad to tell him not to go near the stove because it was hot. No matter how nicely we requested or how deeply we explained the consequences, our son refused to heed our warnings. Finally, as parents sometimes do, I expressed my frustration; "Hot! Get away from there, NOW!" I screamed in exasperation. "If you burn yourself, I don't want to hear a sound out of your mouth!"

A few days later, my wife was preparing dinner on the stove. Sure enough, our son was intentionally putting his hand near the burner. I was sitting in the living room and did not see what he was doing, but I knew my wife was aware when she shouted, "HOT!" A few minutes later, I joined my wife in the kitchen just as our son decided to test the boundaries one last time. He reached up toward the top of the stove, but this time, he accidentally touched the burner. Looking at me helplessly, he covered his mouth with his unburned hand, ran to his room, slammed the door shut, and then screeched and cried in obvious pain and embarrassment.

For our son, he learned a lesson the hard way. Luckily, it was just a minor, first-degree burn. We had tried to teach him that "no meant no," but he would not listen. Our son suffered a painful consequence for not heeding his parents. But he also learned accountability and that the word "no" was a normal part of life.

No and Integrity

When our son touched the stove, we were trying to teach him an important parenting lesson: "No means no!" Unfortunately, many parents do not have the ability to enforce their decisions when they tell their children "No." The easily cave to whining, crying, fits of temper, and adorable "puppy-dog eyes."

We've all been in a store when a child was told that they couldn't have a certain toy or some candy, only to watch as the child throws a tantrum, and the parent simply gives in and buys the child something to appease them. It is difficult to build or maintain personal integrity if we easily submit to avoid confrontation.

By its very nature, the use of the word "no" is confrontational and uncomfortable. Yet it is probably one of the most important words in developing personal integrity. Laws and rules are created to provide behavioral and societal boundaries. When a law says, "No, you cannot do this," we have two choices: We can break the law, or we can obey it. Following laws and rules helps build personal integrity while intentionally disobeying them places a cloud of distrust over us. This is not to suggest that certain laws and rules may not need to be changed over time to keep up with social trends, but overall, laws and rules protect us, often from ourselves.

In general, people do not like to be told what they can and cannot do. This trait is innate; just tell a three-year-old "no" and watch their response. Place a jar of homemade chocolate chip cookies out of reach on the countertop, tell that same three-year-old he/she can't have one, and then leave the room. That child will eventually find a way to climb onto the counter and start eating, and when you return, the child's face will be covered with chocolate smudges. Of course, when asked, the child will deny getting into the cookie jar. Can this be the innocent beginning of how our integrity often crumbles simply because we hear the word "no"?

No and Respect

Once we decide to accept that the word "no" is a normal part of life, we can identify how closely it is tied to our respect of others. How many times have we heard the word "no" and lashed out at the person who dared deny us what we wanted? Three-year-olds often pitch fits in stores when they don't get what they want, and our attitude at hearing the word "no" does not change much as we become adults.

Have we ever asked for a raise from our boss, only to be denied? Suddenly, our demeanor changes, and the boss now becomes the target of our venom. The boss is a "jerk" (or worse), and our disrespect toward this person spreads. We quickly complain to our colleagues and spread disparaging remarks to anyone who will listen.

Unfortunately, bosses don't change who they are simply by uttering a single word, and deep down, we know this to be true. However, we quickly demonstrate our anger and frustration after being told "no," and it clouds our ability to think rationally in the moment. Our emotions take over, and being respectful is the last thing on our minds. We are in pain, so we are going to deflect that pain or at least ensure that our boss feels pain as well. Revenge is not fertile soil for exhibiting respect and damages our personal credibility.

Ironically, in the very moment we are making our derogatory comments about our boss, we are often complaining about the boss's lack of respect for us! Respect is a two-way street, and we should be the ones who exhibit it first, especially when the reason for our personal attack was simply not immediately getting what we want.

Tenet 3 Challenge

For the next ninety days, keep a journal on how other people react when they hear the word "no" or do not get what they want. These people can be coworkers, children, family members, or even supervisors or political leaders. Write down what they were denied and how they responded. Then describe how their reactions affected your perception of their personal accountability, integrity, and respect.

Who was told "no"	Their reaction to being told "no"	How they responded to the offense	How they could avoid taking offense next time

Bonus challenge: Keep a similar journal on how you reacted when you did not get what you wanted. This doesn't have to be something big; it could be something as simple as a child forgetting to do something you asked them to do.

After ninety days, review your journals. What do you notice about the reactions of others when they do not get what they want? Compare and contrast their reactions with yours during that same timeframe. Did you react similarly? Although this may be uncomfortable, be honest here.

TENET 4
Success Is Built on a Foundation of Temporary Setbacks

I've failed over and over again and that is why I succeed.

—Michael Jordan

Building on the message of Tenet 3, Tenet 4 acknowledges the consequences of experiencing "no" in our lives.

The path to success is riddled with potholes, hairpin turns, and steep, seemingly insurmountable uphill climbs. Setbacks are inevitable on the road to success.

Setbacks and Accountability

Perhaps one of the greatest challenges to our personal accountability is how we handle setbacks in life. We must not let temporary setbacks define us, and we must not use them as an excuse to deter us from keeping our commitments.

Every semester, at least one student in my class misses an assignment due to an unforeseen setback. After all, "life happens!" While I do my best to accommodate their situations, sometimes I must draw a line in the sand and hold firm to a deadline. For example, one student (we'll call him Joey, not his real name) missed his writing assignment that was due on a Sunday night. The assignment had been introduced two weeks prior, so there was plenty of time under normal circumstances for any student to meet the deadline. The class met twice a week, on Tuesdays and Thursdays, and Joey had attended every class, so he was completely aware of the Sunday deadline.

When the deadline passed, I received an alert that Joey had not submitted his assignment. Monday passed, but there was no communication from Joey. Tuesday came and went, and this time, Joey was not in class, so I sent an email to check on his well-being. Wednesday also came and went without a word. Finally, on Thursday afternoon, Joey responded to my email. He stated that the reason he missed his assignment was that he got sick on Friday and could not complete it. In that email, he asked for an extension on the deadline. At this point, I could have granted the extension, but what lesson would I be teaching him? After all, he was the only student to miss the deadline. How would that be fair to all the other students?

Instead of responding to his request via email, I waited until class on Thursday to speak with Joey. I first asked how he was feeling, and he abruptly exclaimed he was doing well and asked if he could pass his paper in late.

"So, Joey, you want to turn your paper in late?" I asked halfheartedly.

"Yeah!" he managed to mutter. Joey was a man of few words.

"The problem I have with doing that for you is that you got sick on Friday. But you didn't contact me until today. Were you by chance in the hospital?"

"No, I was just really sick."

"But you didn't leave me a message or send me an email until four days after the assignment was due. Just a quick, 'Hey, Mr. Aldom, I'm really sick' would have at least let me know something was up. If you worked for me and didn't call me for four days, what do you think would happen?"

"You'd fire me. But I was *really* sick," Joey pleaded.

"I believe you were sick, but if you were me, Joey, would *you* give you an extension?"

"Probably not."

While this may have been a hard lesson for Joey to learn, it taught him the importance of personal accountability. He couldn't argue because he knew he had two weeks to write his assignment, and he simply did not communicate when adversity arose.

Two semesters later, Joey popped into my office unexpectedly. He thanked me for my tough love and informed me he retook the class and got an "A."

Setback and Integrity

In the spring of 2010, the first year after my certification, I was hired as a long-term substitute at the high school where I completed my student teaching internship during the prior spring. The instructor was going on maternity leave for the final eight weeks of the semester, and she specifically requested that the district hire me. When I received the call, I was ecstatic. My first long-term teaching job was going to be in the school where I had built several great relationships! I was welcomed back with open arms. The principal and vice principal/athletic director greeted me and assured me that they "had my back." My naivete allowed me to believe that I had the support needed to be successful.

After seven awesome weeks of building relationships with the students using my Fresh A.I.R. classroom management approach, it was time for our end-of-year assessment. Normally, students try to take advantage of substitutes, but from the first day, I let the students know I was not their "typical" substitute. I assured them I am aware of their actions in the classroom. So when it came time to proctor the end-of-course assessment, I informed the students that I expected them to follow our Fresh A.I.R. strategy. As is the case in any classroom, some students will try to bend, stretch, and break the rules whenever they can.

During the test, I watched two of our school's star student athletes turn their chairs inward toward each other when they first sat down. As the test went on, I watched as their eyes wandered ever-so-slightly without moving their heads. Cleverly, they turned in their Scantron sheets separately, but as I graded their test scores, they were identical. Both received an 88/100 on the exam. While identical scores may not be out of the ordinary, as I looked closer, disappointment engulfed me, and my faith in the two students was shattered. Not only were their overall scores identical, so, too, were their entire answer sheets. They got the exact same questions wrong. Moreover, they also changed three questions from right answers to the exact same wrong answers. Even their eraser marks matched up on every question.

I was disheartened, but I didn't want to jump to conclusions. I separately approached three experienced teachers in my department. I did not explain anything; I merely showed them the Scantrons. Immediately, all three teachers, two of whom had over twenty years of experience, told me the students had obviously cheated off each other. Because this was my first encounter with academic dishonesty on a high-stakes test, I asked my mentor teacher what I should do. She told me to do the same thing to our vice principal; do not say anything, just show him the Scantrons.

I immediately walked down to the vice principal's office, and luckily, he was there. I showed him the Scantrons, and he wasted no time in asserting what he believed: "They cheated." When I asked what my role was at this point, he stated matter-of-factly, "I'll handle this. You've done your job. Good job catching this. So what are the students' names?" When I named the two students, the vice principal turned ashen. He realized after hearing the names that these were two of his star athletes. "I'll take care of it" were his final words as I left his office. While I was not thrilled with the fact that two, star athletes had cheated, I felt good that I had protected the academic integrity of the school. Or so I thought.

Because I had first approached three other teachers in the department, word got around that I had caught two students cheating on the exam. One of the teachers was also a head of the department, so she asked the vice principal how we were going to handle the situation given the fact I was a substitute and was on my last day. She was told again that the vice principal would handle the situation.

It was midway through our summer break, and I ran into the department head at the local grocery store. We chatted for a bit, and I asked what action the school decided to take on the two students. In her best Barry White bass voice, she frustratingly forced out just a single word, "Nothing!" I stood there in stunned disbelief as she explained that the students got to keep their scores. No punishment. No retaking of the test. Not even a slap on the wrist. The vice principal (who was also the athletic director) intentionally did nothing and acted as if the event never happened. The parents were not informed. They did not get a zero for the assignment. Absolutely no punishment for academic dishonesty. My eyes must have turned red with rage, and smoke must have been billowing out of my ears because the department head was quick to offer her reassurance, "You did all you could do. It's not on you."

Perhaps the best thing for those two students was for them to receive a failing grade. The lesson they would have learned would have lasted a lifetime. Unfortunately, all the administrator did was reinforce poor decision-making and let the students know that failure was not an option...because he would never allow them to fail even when it was their fault. This was a missed opportunity for the administrator to demonstrate the importance of personal integrity to these students. Instead, the administrator reinforced negative behavior and taught these students that they can cheat and prosper as long as they are athletically gifted.

Setbacks and Respect

Success is built on our ability to overcome failure. In fact, we should consider our setbacks as the rungs in the ladder on which we climb in our journey to success. Each time we reach a new rung, we have overcome setbacks and are now one step closer to our goals. Unfortunately, setbacks often become insurmountable roadblocks that negatively affect not only our success but our self-confidence.

When we have low self-esteem, we lose our confidence and self-respect. Setbacks are often the sparks that ignite low self-esteem. When everything is going well, it is easy to remain optimistic and confident. But when we suffer setbacks, even temporary setbacks, doubt quickly sets in and paralyzes us. Our circle of influence (i.e., our friends and family) notice our idleness and often point to our setback as a reason to quit pursuing our path. This especially happens as setbacks mount. The closer we get to reaching our goals, the steeper the climb, and the easier it can be to lose footing and slip backward.

Unfortunately, our personal setbacks often negatively affect those around us. Eventually, they lose confidence in our ability to succeed, especially when the setbacks are repetitive and frequently self-inflicted. They simply cannot watch as we self-destruct for the tenth time. And who can blame them? No one wants to watch as a loved one continuously fails. Admittedly, my family lived through this during my journey to writing this book.

One of the most difficult experiences I experienced as a parent was watching our oldest son lose every wrestling match his freshman year. When he came home one September day and proudly informed us, "I joined the wrestling team!" I was stunned, and I'm sure my initial expression was less-than-supportive. When I asked him what his goal was, he said he wanted to place at the state tournament by his senior year. I explained to him that most of those kids had been wrestling for years before high school, but he was undeterred.

Deep inside, as his losses mounted, I questioned why he chose this goal. Why did he choose a goal that seemed improbable, if not impossible, especially after a freshman year where he lost every match? But this was *his* goal, not mine. Each loss, each setback, seemed to discourage me more than him.

Normally, when our friends and family give up on us, we lose the very support we often rely on to be successful. Without this support, our self-esteem and dreams quickly dwindle. Ultimately, if not predictably, we give up on the path that defines who we truly are, and accordingly, our self-respect follows.

But our son was different. Even when I tried to talk him out of returning to the wrestling team for his sophomore year, he became more determined than ever to prove me wrong. Despite all the setbacks of his freshman year, and the loss of support and belief of his father, our son never lost focus on his goal. He never let his setbacks destroy his self-respect.

Three years later, as a senior, he placed fourth at the state tournament. In one of the defining moments of our relationship, he walked off the mat after placing in the state tournament, wrapped his sweaty arms tightly around me, and with a bloody smile and tears of joy running down his cheek, proudly exclaimed, "Dad, I just placed at the state tournament!" Mission accomplished!

Tenet 4 Challenge

Identify a goal you once had that you gave up on because your setbacks became roadblocks, so you gave up. Did you lose the support of your friends or family? Or did you give up merely because of a temporary setback?

Next, set a goal that is a stretch for you. Really challenge yourself to achieve something difficult. As you work toward your goal, use a *goal journal* to keep track of your successes and your setbacks. Document your feelings and reactions to your setbacks. How do you feel? Do you want to quit? Have your friends and family given up on you or tried to talk you out of pursuing your goal?

Do not combine the *goal journal* with any daily journal. Keep it separate and focus all your observations on the path to your goal.

TENET 5
Follow Your Passions and True Happiness Will Find You

Death cannot stop true love.

—Westley (played by Cary Elwes) in *The Princess Bride*

While leafing through her grandfather's Bible shortly after he had passed away, my wife found this powerful, handwritten message highlighted in the margins: "The greatest disappointment in life is the difference between who a person is and who they could be!" Perhaps the reason for the gap between who we are and who we could be is that we do not follow our passions.

For many of us, when we remember our first jobs as teenagers, we rarely speak fondly of them. Of course, the viewpoint often did not change as we got older; we begrudgingly worked for low pay and little to no recognition. Even if we excelled at our job, we were rewarded with a twenty-five-cent raise and perhaps a promotion in name only.

To be fair, these first jobs are not usually meant to be our career paths. I remember my first job as an after-school front-end baggage clerk at a local supermarket. I took the job not because I aspired to bag groceries for a living but because, at age fourteen, it was all I was qualified to do. But I was never excited to go to work, especially when I was getting paid $1.75 an hour. In fact, when times were slow and managers asked who wanted to leave early, I often jumped at the opportunity. I did my job well, but it was monotonous. When anyone asked how I felt about my job, I never had anything positive to say. As I look back now, the managers were decent people who treated us with respect. Their jobs were made more difficult because they had to rely on apathetic teenagers to show up as scheduled.

I remember complaining to my grandfather one day about hating my job and how it was the worst job ever. He laughed and proceeded to tell me about how he was cleaning soot out of smokestacks as a teenager. What could I say? As I swallowed that giant piece of humble pie, my grandfather then relayed the most life-altering work advice, "No job is beneath you. Don't you *ever* let your employer regret he gave you a paycheck!"

His admonition changed my view about work forever. I stayed with my job for another three years and never forgot my grandfather's sage words. I matured, became more reliable, and suddenly the managers increased my responsibilities. I became more accountable, and my managers noticed.

Passion and Accountability

When we are truly passionate about our activities, careers, or relationships, we tend to focus our dedication and efforts. Accordingly, our passion then positively impacts our personal accountability. After all, when we are chasing what really drives us, we are less likely to let anything derail us. It becomes more difficult to miss deadlines or simply give up.

Think back to a time when you achieved a goal that required a dedicated effort on your part. Reflect on the diligence you exhibited as you pursued that goal. How often did you hold yourself accountable along the way?

For the first twelve years of my marriage, I held numerous sales jobs. I always performed well, but with the exception of one job at a family-owned car dealership, I was never passionate about any of these jobs. It was not long before I would become bored and dissatisfied.

When I accepted the job at that family-owned dealership in the fall of 2001, my attitude changed. From day 1, they treated me with respect. I was a person, not just a dispensable employee. My second month was particularly rough; I sold one car on the first day and did not sell another car until the last day of the month. I had written thirteen deals, but twelve of the deals fell through in finance. I could not catch a break.

Right after our morning meeting on that last day of the month, the owner sat down near my desk. I was terrified because when you have a terrible month like I had, it usually means you are about to be fired. I am quite certain he could feel my anxiety, and as he started speaking, I was waiting for him to ask me to pack up my desk. Instead, to my surprise, he just smiled and said, "Rough month, huh? Don't worry, you'll make up for it next month. Just give me your best today."

My jaw must have bounced off the floor. No scolding. No threatening my job. No firing. Just words of encouragement. Suddenly, I was calm and full of confidence. And it showed as I sold two cars on that last day of the month.

On that day, I made a vow to be the top salesperson within the next six months. This seemed like an insurmountable goal considering there were two salespeople who had worked for the company for over twenty-five years each. But I was now passionate about my job and where I worked. I was willing to do whatever it took to achieve my goal. Each day, I held myself accountable by vowing to be the first salesperson to arrive and the last to leave each day. I kept my promise, and it paid off; three months later, I was salesperson of the month!

The owner's words had changed my mind about my job. For the next two years, I never missed a scheduled day of work. Instead of just going through the motions, I took my job seriously.

Passion and Integrity

While working at that dealership I was introduced to the concept that passion and integrity are inextricably connected, although their relationship may not be initially apparent.

On the first day working at the dealership, while sitting down and arranging my desk, I was approached by a man I had never seen before. I looked up and offered a rather unconfident, "Can I help you find someone in particular?" He graciously smiled and sat down. It was the owner, but I didn't know it yet. His only words were, "Keep doing what you're doing. Don't mind me."

I decided to make small talk with my visitor, and then the manager casually walked by and identified the visitor by name. It was the owner! *But he's so down-to-earth*, I thought quizzically. His soft-spoken nature did not coincide with his position of authority. Until that point in my life, every business owner was forceful, aggressive, and authoritarian. Perhaps I expected the owner to be formal and gruff, and at the time, I was quite intimidated meeting the man whose name was on the building.

I expected my visitor to follow the manager to his office, but he just sat at my desk and resumed our discussion. The more we talked, the more I felt his passion for cars and his business. Twenty minutes later, after our pleasant, unexpected conversation, the owner stood up. He started walking away but turned back and made an unexpected request, "Whatever you do, please do not tarnish my name. No shady stuff, okay?"

His words caught me off guard. I had never had my integrity questioned in this manner. But it made sense. He had spent years chasing his passion and built a reputation of integrity and trust. I never considered how my integrity had the capacity to negatively impact the integrity of another person.

Nearly two decades later, I still remember my first encounter with this principled man whom I came to admire and respect. His passion was contagious, and his integrity was unimpeachable. Although the connection of passion and integrity is undeniable, I am not certain whether it was his integrity that drove his passion or vice versa. But it was my relationship with this man that clearly taught me how, in certain circumstances, passion and integrity are inextricably connected.

Passion and Respect

At that point in my life, I had never personally met a person with more passion for his career than the owner of that dealership. His passion infected me, and it drove me to be a better employee for him. How could I not respect a person who puts his heart and soul into his work as much as this man did?

When we follow our passions, respect often becomes an unintentional by-product of our efforts. As we follow our true path in life, our work ethic intensifies. Nothing will prevent us from achieving these goals, so we tend to work more diligently and tirelessly to obtain them. Our self-worth is often attached to our ability to work, and there is a certain level of satisfaction we experience when we accomplish even the smallest task.

Admittedly, Tenet 5 was the most challenging for me. My passion has always been writing, even when I wasn't consciously aware of its importance in my life. Unfortunately, I never followed my true passion until now. The further I got from my passion, the less I respected myself. I was a fraud, and there was no way I could respect a fraud.

Eventually, I found inspiration from my wife. She chased her passion, and her joy is evident. She is well respected in the education realm and has assisted in writing and editing postsecondary textbooks, developed entire course curricula used by a consortium of colleges and universities throughout the state, and is a respected voice at her college. Her passion is evident, and the respect she receives is a by-product of her passion.

My steps to gain respect began by offering my writing and editing services online. I dipped my toes lightly to avoid becoming overwhelmed. The more my services were used online, the more I enjoyed the path I was on…the path toward chasing my passion.

Before long, I transitioned from focusing on my small online projects to writing books. Along the way, I rediscovered my self-respect, simply by focusing on my passion.

Tenet 5 Challenge

Identify your top three passions in life and write them down. Is your career tied to one of your passions? If not, evaluate how happy you are in your current career. If you are unhappy, perhaps now is the time to make the change.

Develop a plan that incorporates your true passion into your career. If it requires more education, then develop a plan to return to school. Set a firm start date. Then start.

If further education is not needed, develop a transition plan that will pave the way to turning your passion into your career. Write this plan down.

Finally, make a list of the top five to ten people who you know will support you as you turn your passion into your career.

Note: This transition will be difficult. Life will definitely hand place roadblocks in your way. It is not a matter of "if" roadblocks will appear as much as a matter of "when." Only surround yourself with those who will help you overcome those roadblocks on your path.

TENET 6
Success Is Ours to Define!

There are two types of people who will tell you that you
cannot make a difference in this world: those who are
afraid to try and those who are afraid you will succeed.

—Ray Goforth

After high school, I took a couple of years off before I attended college. When I finally decided to apply, there was no shortage of career suggestions offered by friends and family. Everyone had their own definition of success, but most of their suggestions only focused on how much money I could make. My mind swam as I considered the infinite opportunities each college offered. When I applied, I did not choose wisely. I settled on accounting as my major, but this was a huge mistake at that time; I had absolutely no passion for accounting.

I had let others convince me that earning an accounting degree was a respectable way to achieve success, but whose definition of success was it? I quickly had no desire to pursue the accounting degree, and predictably, I dropped out of college after the first semester. I had let everyone else define my path to success, and I was miserable.

It took another three years before I decided to give college another try. But once again, I let others determine my path. This time, I was convinced to pursue a degree in metallurgy. The major professor was definitely passionate about metallurgy, and I got caught up in his enthusiasm. Once again, after just one semester, I knew I was pursuing the wrong degree. Instead of dropping out, I decided to spend the next two semesters focusing on the core courses and electives I would need to graduate. To ease my sense of failure, I assured myself, "You have two semesters to figure things out!"

Unfortunately, after I completed those semesters, I was no closer to choosing a major. Every option that others suggested was uninspiring. It never dawned on me that I was taking a passive approach to my pursuit of success. I was letting everyone except me define my path to success. I once again dropped out of college, and this time, I did not return for another decade!

During my second hiatus from college, I decided it was best to support my wife's decision to pursue her degree. It was a gamble; we had to move five hundred miles so she could attend school. Ironically, her first semester was much like mine. After working for several years as a pharmacy technician, she had returned to school with the plan of becoming a pharmacist. The most appealing aspects of pursuing her pharmacology degree were that she would make a high income, work a flexible schedule, and be home with our children when they got out of school each day.

When she completed her first semester, in fact, the day she completed her last final exam, my wife came home in tears. When I asked her what was wrong, with a hint of fear and anxiety in her voice, she choked out her reply, "I don't want to be a pharmacist." I was stunned; we had moved five hundred miles for her to pursue her pharmacy degree!

"But you were the one who said you wanted to be a pharmacist," I retorted without the slightest hint of support in my voice. "You liked being a pharmacy technician, and a pharmacist makes so much more money. What's the problem?"

"I don't know," she bawled. "I just don't want to be a pharmacist."

"Well, then, what *do* you want?" I blurted sarcastically.

"I've always wanted to be a teacher," she conceded apprehensively.

My heart softened. I realized that my wife, in her vulnerable state, was trusting me to support her decision. It would require a huge leap of faith on both our parts. "Are you sure that's what you want to do?" I prodded. Her countenance immediately changed as she assured me it had always been her dream.

My uncertainty was still churning inside, so I interrogated her like she was on trial for her life. We discussed the decision in depth, including important aspects such as the difference in income, the additional coursework she would need to take because she was changing her degree, and where we might live after she graduated. Despite my incessant questions, my wife became more certain that she wanted to chase her dream…*her dream!* Not my dream.

It finally hit me. My wife wanted to become a teacher. It wasn't about the money. It wasn't about prestige, fame, or fortune. It was all about chasing her dream, *her passion!*

Success and Accountability

One of the most difficult parts of chasing our dreams is the realization that we alone are ultimately in charge of our success…or failure. Along the way, life's challenges will inevitably knock us off our envisioned pathway. I often call this the scenic route to achieving our goals. All too often, these unforeseen detours become the rationales, or more appropriately, the excuses for giving up on our dreams.

It is during these difficult struggles that we need the courage to hold firm to our personal accountability. Why? Because when the path to our dreams becomes rocky, it becomes all too easy to search for scapegoats. And when scapegoats are not people, it becomes easier to fall into the self-destructive snare of blaming "fate" for our failures. After all, "fate" is faceless. We can't see its ugly head when life's trials occur, nor can we see its beauty when blessings come our way. While it is true that certain events or circumstances in life are beyond our control, for the most part, we still have the autonomy to overcome these roadblocks.

By understanding how truly important it is to embrace accountability as a character trait, we place ourselves in a mindset that refuses to lose. Being accountable to our own actions, thoughts, and decisions strengthens our ability to overcome adversity by forcing us to look inward for strength instead of outward for excuses. Frequently, when we look inward, we convince ourselves we do not have the power to conquer the obstacles before us. This occurs when our personal accountability is actually at its weakest. When our lives become worn down by outside forces, we begin to doubt our inner strength. Personal accountability slowly and methodically fades away from our character.

The path to writing this book is a perfect example of "the scenic route" toward achieving a dream. Job instability, self-doubt, family obligations, pandemic, and societal upheaval all distracted my focus and weakened my personal accountability. Instead of keeping my eyes on the goal, I allowed outside forces to erode my personal accountability. The "blame game" crept in, and I became trapped in a mental web filled with "Why try?" and "No one cares."

When it looked as if I was just about to scrap this whole idea of writing a book, I was given the opportunity to speak in a small setting about any topic I wanted. I chose some of the foundational aspects of Fresh A.I.R., and after I spoke, several people approached me and thanked me for giving them the hope to chase their dreams once again. This one small success sparked my personal accountability pilot light. I realized that I had allowed outside forces to become the scapegoats for my setbacks.

Ironically, when we find successes after facing hardships, no matter how small or seemingly insignificant they are, they become the scaffolding for even bigger achievements. Our enthusiasm grows; our belief that we can achieve our dreams is reborn. Our personal accountability once again becomes a powerful character trait that drives us toward our dreams.

Success and accountability are fundamentally intertwined, for good and bad. Inevitably, personal accountability will drive us toward success when it is a character strength or become the excuse for our failures when abandoned.

Success and Integrity

A popular quote by sports coaches is, "If you ain't cheating, you ain't trying." But should that be our personal mantra when chasing our dreams? Should we chase our dreams with blindness, stepping on anyone or anything that may get in our way?

In order to achieve true success, we should not forfeit our morality. This is especially true during times of personal struggle. We should not give in to the "Robin Hood" mentality: doing the wrong thing for the right reasons. Despite having altruistic intentions, when we sacrifice our integrity to achieve success, whether we want to admit it or not, we diminish the power of our accomplishment.

Remember the two athletes in Tenet 4 who cheated yet were not disciplined by the vice principal and were allowed to keep their final grade? The vice principal was convinced his decision was correct because, after all, he did not want to ruin the chances of his star athletes competing in college. In his mind, he was doing the wrong thing for the right reasons.

He justified his decision, but at what cost? The educators affected by the vice principal's decision never forgot, especially me. It wasn't a teacher who made the decision, but rather an administrator and athletic director who allowed himself to rationalize a wrong decision while sacrificing his personal integrity. While his star players achieved individual athletic success the following year, the vice principal lost all his credibility with several teachers.

When our youth leaders, mentors, and role models encourage cheating and dishonesty to achieve success under the guise of Robin Hood ethics, the negative effects ripple for generations. The vice principal's actions did not only affect those involved at that moment. Yes, his actions instilled unfavorable moral justification in the athletes. More importantly, the vice principal caused a new teacher to become jaded toward the entire educational system. Other teachers involved realized this administrator did not have their backs. The vice principal was willing to do the wrong thing to justify his decisions, and once that occurred, his integrity was lost forever.

Robin Hood was a thief, not a hero, no matter what excuses we use to justify his actions. Doing the wrong thing for the right reasons means we still did the wrong thing. We can justify doing wrong, but just like the vice principal, we must ask ourselves, "At what cost?"

Success and Respect

One of the most difficult challenges of pursuing and obtaining our personal success is the ability to maintain respect during and after the journey. Unfortunately, many of today's role models rely on self-aggrandizing public behavior once they obtain success. This behavior is in total contrast to the definition of respect. Why is this egocentric behavior worthy of high regard?

The greatest successes in human history stand the test of time, and the authors of those successes are often held in the highest esteem. Yet history rarely describes those architects as arrogant. Imagine some of the greatest historical figures publicly gloating about their accomplishments.

For example, would Abraham Lincoln or George Washington be held in as high regard today had they boasted about their accomplishments before, during, and after they became presidents? Can we imagine Thomas Edison running around thumping his chest after each patent he obtained? With over one thousand patents to his name, Edison was one of the most prolific inventors in history. Similarly, Benjamin Franklin's inventive contributions have stood the test of time. Together, their creative accomplishments truly benefited mankind and were worthy of recognition, more so than any personal athletic achievement.

Some will argue that in order to succeed, we must have a chip on our shoulders. Indeed, we need confidence to succeed, but that does not mean we must exude it at the expense of others. There is a fine line between confidence and arrogance, and I argue that confidence comes from within, but arrogance is the pretentious outward manifestation of inner confidence. The only person who gains anything by boasting of their accomplishments is the braggart.

This is not to say that there are no athletes worthy of our respect. We have been blessed in the past half century with athletes who remained humble despite all their personal successes: David Robinson, Tim Duncan, Larry Fitzgerald, and Cal Ripken Jr. to name a few. Although their legacies and accomplishments were noteworthy, during interviews with the media, can we ever remember when they focused entirely on themselves? Everyone saw what they accomplished, yet when they were placed in the spotlight, they deflected praise to teammates, coaches, and even to their God. These players earned respect because they always displayed respect, especially when the spotlight was shining on them.

Cal Ripken Jr. broke a record everyone thought was unbreakable when he passed Lou Gehrig's all-time consecutive games-played record in 1995. On September 6, Ripken played in his 2,131st consecutive game, a phenomenal feat that will most likely never be broken because modern athletes are now scheduled rest days numerous times every season. When the game became official after the fifth inning, Ripken reluctantly participated in the celebration that followed.

His victory lap around Camden Yards in Baltimore was encouraged, more accurately, forced, by his teammates; and he was visibly overwhelmed and humbled in the moment. Now imagine that same celebration with Ripken running around the ballpark, thumping his chest, telling the world he was the greatest of all time.

On that day, Ripken cemented his legacy, a legacy built on humility and respect. His legacy will never be tarnished due to a selfish, egocentric display when he succeeded. Instead, Ripken's legacy will endure because he chose, in his greatest moment, to share his success with humility and respect.

Tenet 6 Challenge

Identify a previous personal success. Now determine whether it was truly your success, or did you merely fulfill someone else's goal they defined for you?

Next, take the goal you identified in Tenet 4 (your "stretch" goal) and picture what it will be like in the moment when you reach that goal (succeed). Now describe what that moment will be like. With whom will you share the success? How will you react? Will you remain respectful and humble, or will you get caught up in the moment?

Finally, define success for yourself from this day forward. What does it look like? What achievement will define your personal success? What steps will be required? Write down all the steps, then place a specific date when you will achieve each step.

TENET 7
Effort: "Leave it all on the mat!"

Nothing worth having was ever achieved without effort.

—Theodore Roosevelt

Following in the footsteps of their older brother, our other two sons decided to test the waters and join the wrestling team. As is often the case, sibling rivalry was often a great motivator. Each brought different skillsets to the table.

Our eldest was a defensive-minded, counteroffensive wrestler. He usually waited until his opponent attempted a move, and then he would react accordingly. Defensive-style wrestlers are not usually embraced by their coaches, and my son's coach was no different. Wrestling coaches teach aggression and offense, and for the most part, it does create the most successful wrestlers. Unfortunately, during his first year of wrestling, our eldest focused all his time during practice learning new offensive moves. He was overwhelmed trying to learn every new move, and he grew increasingly frustrated because he believed he thought he needed to know all the wrestling holds perfectly, and when things didn't work out as he had practiced, he was lost, both literally and figuratively.

One day after practice, he was particularly agitated at the events that unfolded. He was trying certain moves, and they were not working. Instead of gaining control, my son was finding himself being reversed or pinned. He wanted to give up because those certain holds were not working for him. It was at this point that we came up with a different game plan.

I asked him if there were any moves he felt comfortable with, and he listed three to four holds he thought he could use. I then suggested he master just those holds instead of being knowledgeable about hundreds of moves. He was quick to question my suggestion, so I explained our new game plan: We would wrestle every match to his strengths. He would only use the holds he mastered, and he would make his opponent wrestle to his strengths. "That won't work!" he argued. I held firm to my suggestion, and his reply was even more adamant, "That's stupid! You can't win with just a few holds!"

I explained, albeit in a frustrated tone from his defeatist mentality, that if he bought into my suggestion, we could then focus more time on defending the moves that other wrestlers used against him. "Trust me," I begged. "Just master a few holds and leave it all on the mat!" In that moment, Tenet 7 was born!

Effort and Accountability

My son begrudgingly agreed to mastering a few holds. He would learn the basics during practice, and we would expand on what he learned when he came home. We discussed what worked, what didn't work, and how we could improve the hold to work under difficult circumstances. At first, improvements came slowly. My son insisted he was giving it his all at practice, but he showed limited success using those holds at the meets and tournaments, mostly because he was hesitant while wrestling top-seeded wrestlers. It was difficult to gauge improvement when his matches usually ended within the first minute or two.

After a quick defeat, my son came off the mat and quasi-dejectedly asserted, "Oh well. I did my best."

I offered a harsh, two-word response: "Did you?" His demeanor immediately changed to anger and frustration because I questioned his accountability. And while most people would argue my response was cold and uncaring, and truthfully it probably was, I wanted him to analyze his match deeper than just a superficial, "Oh well. I lost." I wanted him to find something he did well, something he did not do well, and something we could build on.

What I did not want was for my son to simply accept defeat nonchalantly. If losing was not painful to him, he would never truly seek to improve. If he did not search for ways to overcome adversity, then every roadblock in life would prevent him from reaching his goals. And we had a daunting goal he set with a short time frame: within four years, he wanted to place at the state tournament.

My response, although severe and antagonistic, elicited the emotional investment I was hoping for. His response showed both of us that he would not be satisfied just "going through the motions." He was fully invested in achieving his goal, and as difficult as it would be, I would continue to challenge his accountability. Before every match, I repeatedly parroted, "Leave it all on the mat!"

As each wrestling season progressed, my son's understanding of the importance of personal accountability increased. We watched as he matured from his freshman superficial response of "Oh, well" to his senior-year introspection, "I should have done this." It was most apparent in his demeanor when he came off the mat after a loss. In his first two years, as he grew to understand accountability, he would be angry, agitated, and would often clash with his parents after losing a match. But as a senior, if he didn't leave it all on the mat, he would simply avoid us. Our son knew what we would say, and deep down, he knew if we had watched him not give his all, we would call him to the carpet.

Effort is the key to embracing personal accountability. When we come up short in achieving our goals, do we look for excuses? Do we evaluate our performance objectively? In the end, there is one question we must ask ourselves that will determine whether we were truly accountable, "Did I leave it all on the mat?"

Effort and Integrity

Integrity is not a passive character trait; on the contrary, it takes conscious effort to establish personal integrity, especially when society continues to downplay its importance.

Social media users are quick to glorify dishonest, illegal activity. Videos of people breaking into stores and stealing simply because the perpetrators claim to be victims are flouted. Witnesses in the streets egg on the wannabe Robin Hoods as they steal cell phones, electronics, and clothes. Suddenly, we are bombarded by criminals reverting to the "If you ain't cheatin', you ain't tryin'" mentality being portrayed as heroes. But if we question their integrity and call them out for being criminals, we are criticized for not understanding their predicament in life. Or we are labeled as "judgmental."

As with all high school sports, wrestling is filled with instances of student athletes taking short cuts to succeed. Our middle son encountered a specific team whose coach encouraged their wrestlers to head-slap as a way to get their opponents off guard. The same coaches also taught to use an illegal cross-face, moving their arm outward and then intentionally (and illegally) slamming their forearms across their opponents' faces with excessive force.

My son came home from a meet bruised across his face and head. He was angry, and rightfully so. He had been assaulted by illegal wrestling maneuvers, and apparently, the referees did nothing to stop it when he complained to them. "What am I supposed to do?" he demanded.

My response, admittedly, was not full of integrity, "If they do it to you, do it back to them…only harder!" I unexpectedly learned the true value of integrity from my son that day when he replied, "Dad, I'm not going to cheat." His response left me humbled…and a bit humiliated. What was my response teaching him about *my* integrity? In that moment, I forgot what integrity was and became Robin Hood.

Throughout all their nine combined years of wrestling, our sons wrestled with integrity. They shook every coach's hand, they shook every referee's hand before and after the match, they shook every opponent's hand whether they won or lost, and they refused to cheat even when some of their opponents cheated. One wrestler even punched our eldest son on the mat at the district tournament. The referee told my son he was going to disqualify his opponent, but my son told the referee he would beat him on the mat. The referee deducted two points from the wrestler and let the match continue. And although he would have been justified in retaliating, my son chose the high road and won on the mat.

Watching my sons overcome adversity on the mat taught me the importance of maintaining integrity no matter the situation. While it would have been easier, if not justified, to retaliate, they chose to do what was right, even in defeat.

A few years after he graduated from high school and stopped wrestling, our son called from college. He wanted to tell us what he did that day, and we could hear the pride in his voice. Apparently, he went to the bank to withdraw some money from the ATM, and as most college students understand, he only had limited funds in his account. As he tried to withdraw $20, the ATM spit out hundreds of dollars more. The receipt showed he requested $20, so he had not punched in the wrong amount. Obviously, he had less money in his account than what the ATM spewed.

We asked him what he did next, and he said he drove right around to the front door, went in the bank, showed him his receipt, and told them what happened. The teller brought the bank manager over, and my son repeated his story to the bank manager. Incredulously, she thanked my son for his honesty and integrity and told him most people would have just driven off with the money.

Most parents attempt to establish strong character in their children. We were no different. When our son called and told us his story, we were grateful and extremely humbled. His honesty and integrity had been tested, and he aced the test. Parents hope for the best, but until their children are tested on their own, parents will never know their true character.

The losses…the cheating…those fade with time. But establishing unwavering integrity on and off the mat…that is timeless.

Effort and Respect

Because respect is earned, it is easy to see how effort and respect are connected. We cannot expect others to respect us while we sit idly on the sidelines. Respect is even harder to garner after we have made a mistake.

At the district tournament his senior year, our oldest son was wrestling in the third-place match. The winner of this match was guaranteed a place at the state tournament while the loser would have to hope to be chosen as an unseeded wild card entrant. He was just a few short minutes from achieving his dream of making it to the state tournament. He was leading by one point with less than ten seconds left. Then inexplicably, the referee called stalling twice in the last ten seconds, giving the opponent a point, tying the match, and sending it to overtime.

Before overtime, the referee explained to the scorekeeper the two calls for stalling, claiming there was no offensive move by our son. However, there was video of our son making at least one offensive move during that timeframe, which would have negated at least one of the stall calls. I was livid, and my wife was deeply disheartened by the decision.

The match went to sudden death, and our son lost. Unless he was granted the one wild card spot, he would not achieve his dream of placing at the state tournament.

The next week, our son was informed that he was granted the wild card and would be going to the state tournament. As fate would have it, while walking into the arena, our son crossed paths with the referee of his district tournament match. Then, the unimaginable happened.

The referee approached our son, stuck out his hand to shake, and humbly apologized, "I am so sorry I missed that call at districts. And I'm really glad you are here because you deserve it. Good luck." My wife and I were stunned. Most referees we have encountered are aloof, yet this one went out of his way to approach our son to apologize.

We gained profound respect for that referee that day. With his concerted effort to reach out to our son and apologize, he earned our respect. He could have simply ignored our son's presence or avoided him altogether at the tournament. But he showed both integrity and respect in his actions, and our perspective for him will be changed forever.

At the district tournament, we lost all respect for someone we barely knew. However, only one short week later, with intentional effort, this referee exemplified how effort and respect are irrevocably intertwined and taught us a lesson in integrity and respect we can never forget.

Tenet 7 Challenge

Tenet 7 takes *effort*: It's time for action; *leave it all on the mat!*

Now that you have embraced the new you, the final challenge is to live the Fresh A.I.R. tenets daily. Every day, when faced with trials, setbacks, and societal influence, we need to remain alert. As society constantly changes, we need to identify the ever-changing, suffocating weapons of negativity, divisiveness, hostility, and pessimism and consciously fight their effects. When faced with these challenges, remember how good Fresh A.I.R. feels, and then BREATHE.

*B*elieve in yourself.

*R*efuse to participate in gossiping and bullying.

*E*liminate negativity.

*A*void bandwagons.

*T*urn from hate.

*H*elp those in need.

*E*ncourage others.

The First Breath: *B*elieve in Yourself

This first breath of Fresh A.I.R. is a bit scary. Just like a newborn infant, you enter this new mindset wary of your shortcomings and reliant upon others to help guide you through this change. You must first believe you can change before change can occur. If you have a fixed mindset and do not believe you can change, then stop now because you will not change. Change requires a growth mindset, and growth is uncomfortable. This is what makes breathing Fresh A.I.R. difficult. Your belief will determine your success.

Quite frequently, the biggest stumbling block to believing in ourselves is the unexpected, sudden onset of impostor syndrome. Just when we seem to be headed for success, self-doubt engulfs us. Our brains become filled with false narratives such as, "I don't belong." Or maybe "They are going to find out I'm a fraud." When these thoughts creep in, we often become paralyzed and instead of moving forward, we quit. The debilitating effects of impostor syndrome can cripple even the most focused individual.

I once was approached by a nontraditional student (we'll call him Bill, not his real name) after he graduated with his bachelor's degree in biology. He explained that he had just been hired as an entry-level lab technician at a local medical center and wanted to know if I would write a letter of recommendation for him...for graduate school!

I was Bill's teacher in his first class when he returned to college at the age of forty. I spent the first day covering the course syllabus and reviewing the semester's assignments. After class, Bill approached me and told me that he was going to quit college and that he made a huge mistake deciding to return to school. I smiled at him and calmly asked, "Am I your first class back?" He struggled to maintain eye contact but managed a sheepish "Yes...there's no way I can do all this by the end of the semester."

I replied with a bold demand, "Don't quit. You *can* do it. I promise if you come to class prepared every day, put in an honest effort, and come to me the moment you have any questions, you will succeed. Give me one month. If you are failing after one month, you can withdraw. Just give me a month. All I ask is that you promise to put in the effort. Remember, you belong, Bill." He apprehensively agreed.

By the end of the semester, Bill's countenance had changed drastically. He attended every class, and instead of looking sullen and hunched over when he arrived, he was beaming with confidence.

But this was not the first time as an educator I had encountered someone with a severe case of impostor syndrome who wanted to quit chasing his dream after the first day. I was working as a consultant in the writing center at the same school the year prior when a formal military serviceman trudged in and sunk his defeated body in the chair across from me. He, too, was over forty years old, and he had just lost his job three weeks before the semester began. Luckily, he had VA benefits that would pay for his schooling.

Jake (not his real name) was initially excited to return to school and earn the degree in engineering he had always wanted. However, he had just received his grade on his first essay: a D-. He shoved the paper in front of me, and with tears rolling down his cheeks, he blurted, "You can't help me, but my instructor said to visit the writing center." The writing center worked on an appointment system, but Jake did not know and had just showed up unannounced. Coincidentally, my appointment that was due at that very moment called in and rescheduled to a later time. I do not believe in coincidences; Jake was supposed to be my appointment all along.

"Jake, do you truly believe I can't help you?" I uneasily asked, taken aback by his emotional state.

"I can't write. I've failed at English my whole life. Everyone has tried to help me, and no one could. There ain't anything you can do that someone else hasn't tried!"

"Well, Jake, I'd like to try, if that's okay? But before we begin, what do you think are your biggest problems with English or writing?"

"Commas and grammar. Oh, and my ideas are always scattered…I just can't make my papers make sense. I can't get what's in my mind on the paper." Jake's frustration grew just talking about his challenges.

"I can help you, Jake. I know I can. But you have to first *believe* I can help you. I know others haven't been able to help, but I won't quit on you if you don't quit on me. Deal?"

"I guess."

At that point, I decided that focusing on the paper was not the best path at this point of our relationship, so I changed the subject. If I was going to help Jake, I needed to know who he was at his core. I asked him about his military career, his love of engineering, and his journey back to school.

Perhaps the most disheartening story Jake told was how it was English teachers who destroyed his confidence to become better at English. As an English instructor, I felt ashamed as he relayed event after event where English teachers humiliated him in front of the class.

By the end of our appointment, we learned we had a few things in common. Jake even cracked a smile as he got up to leave.

"When are you here?" Jake asked, this time with a little optimism in his voice.

"Check the front desk. They have my schedule and know what appointment slots are available."

"Thanks, man," Jake offered as he left.

"We got this!" I bellowed.

Both Jake and Bill were overcome with impostor syndrome the first time their dreams were met with opposition. They lacked belief in their own abilities to overcome challenges. While I knew I had the ability and background to assist them with their writing skills, I knew if I did not change their mindsets, they would not succeed. They needed to *believe* before we could work toward reaching their goals.

Bill and Jake were two of my proudest moments as an educator and reinforced why I chose education as a career. I attended their graduations, and I felt almost as proud of them as I did when my own children graduated.

Unfortunately, impostor syndrome is like the common cold. It can be dormant for a long time, but when we least expect it, it recurs. When Bill came in asking for the recommendation letter for graduate school, I could tell impostor syndrome was settling in. "I doubt I'll get into the school I want. I just hope I'll have some school accept me."

"Bill, you are doing it again. What makes you think you won't get in? What did I tell you that first day?"

"I belong," he responded with a hint of embarrassment.

I wrote Bill's letter of recommendation to his top three schools, and he was accepted to all three. Bill recently completed his master's degree in microbiology. He battled impostor syndrome the entire way. But in the end, Bill became who he was always meant to be. It wasn't my content knowledge in English that helped Bill and Jake to succeed.

I taught them to take the first breath of Fresh A.I.R. I taught them to *believe*!

The Second Breath: *R*efuse to Participate in Bullying

The advent and meteoric rise of social media has lent itself to an increase in bullying. What is the intended outcome of bullying? Think about it: If someone's goal is to intentionally either physically or emotionally harm another human being, how purely evil is that mentality, especially when it is directed at people who usually cannot defend themselves.

If you are prone to bullying others, including passive-aggressive behaviors such as gossiping, ask yourself, "Why do I enjoy intentionally hurting others? Does this behavior truly make me happy? What if I suddenly became the target of bullying?"

In my youth, I remember my siblings were the victim of constant bullying from four particular families in our neighborhood. My older brother, who had serious health issues, bore the brunt of most of the bullying. These families picked on him incessantly, mostly because of his small, frail stature. In school, I remember my siblings being the targets of constant ridicule.

Admittedly, I was occasionally bullied, but most of the bullying toward me was mild compared to my brother. I was picked on because of academic achievement more than anything. But I was also quite athletic and could defend myself when challenged. My brother, on the other hand, was physically limited, so he was an easy target.

One day after school, when I was ten or eleven years old, in an unbelievably brazen act, one member of the four families that bullied my brother came into our yard and for no reason shoved my brother to the ground. We had a rather large yard, about an acre, so I ran across the yard screaming for my oldest brother to help. By the time I returned with my oldest brother, the bully was on the ground, crying in pain. Apparently, something happened at school earlier in the day, and my brother had decided he had enough of the bullying. The bully claimed he was going to come to our house and "kick his…" This time, my brother was ready. He defended himself. For that one day, my brother was no longer a victim of bullying.

Back then, bullying was somewhat common, and it usually ended when someone stood up to the bully. But times have changed. Bullying is no longer simply a physical act. It has evolved into an emotional weapon that leaves scars that outlast any of the physical ones left behind after standing up to the bully.

The rise of social media and cell phone cameras have made it easier to spread bullying. The sad reality is that bullying has become even more prevalent in society in the past half century. And its newest form comes from a computer screen. Bullying is now indelible; threats violence and insults are now permanently uploaded to Facebook, X, TikTok, and other social platforms in real time.

Online gossiping, threats, and insults are now the weapons of choice for bullies. The internet has become a haven for those who would not normally have the courage to spread gossip or throw insults in person. These bullies hide behind their keyboards, safe from any direct, physical confrontation. Their harmful words are easy to spew because they are directed at a computer screen and not directly at their target. No visible, physical scars are being left, so the bullies do not realize, or do not care, about the emotional damage they are inflicting.

Perhaps the real cause of the rise in bullying, whether physical or emotional, is the change in how society deals with bullying, especially in the educational system.

In previous generations, bullies in school were punished harshly. They were usually suspended, with the suspensions becoming increasingly longer for repeat offenders. Nowadays, in an incomprehensible and undefendable act of ignorance, the public education system has determined that if a victim stands up to the person bullying them, they give the same punishment to the victim as the bully. Moreover, neither child is removed from the school. They serve "in-school suspensions."

Several years ago, when our second son was in middle school, he came home after school almost in tears. He slammed his backpack down and said he hated school. When we asked what was wrong, he described months of bullying by a particular student. We were in shock. "Why don't you go to the principal?" my wife asked in a mixed tone of one part love and one part frustration." His response was even more appalling: "I have!" he yelled in an equally irritated fashion. "Three times! And he won't do anything about it."

While we had taught our children to never start a fight, we had also told them to never become a victim of bullying. I told my son as long as he didn't start or antagonize someone into a fight, he had the right to defend himself. But if I found out he was the instigator, he would be in more trouble. He promised he had done nothing to warrant the bullying. I told him to avoid the bully as much as possible, but it didn't take long for the bully to strike again.

The very next day, while our son was out in the hall taking a test, the bully snuck up from behind and yanked the chair out from under our son. He hit his head on the desk, and his test paper went flying. This time, our son decided it was time to defend himself. And he did.

I received a call from the vice principal about the incident. He explained the incident, so I asked if the other person was the specific student my son had complained about just a day earlier. The vice principal said he could not divulge the student's name and offered a stern rebuke, "We're very disappointed that your son has chosen to work out his problems in a physical nature."

I'm certain my disgust and sarcasm were palpable when I responded, "Maybe he would not have responded with physicality if you had listened when he came to you three times to tell you he was being bullied!"

So why does bullying have a stronghold on our collective psyches? Has society become so depraved that it now embraces bullying as some sort of heroic act? Some find scapegoats for the glorifying of physical violence in violent video games or mixed martial arts. Others will look for emotional or psychological rationales. Regardless, the trend of encouraging, endorsing, or participating in bullying, whether physical or emotional, must be reversed.

The next time you come upon someone gossiping or bullying another person, stop and remember to take your second breath of Fresh A.I.R. and refuse to participate.

The Third Breath: *E*liminate Negativity

Much of the impetus to write this book came from personal introspection and a realization of the author's own shortcomings. As a child, I was brimming with optimism. The world was filled with wonders, and I was enamored by what was possible.

But as is the case with many people, as I grew, I allowed myself to become overwhelmed by cynicism. Over the course of many years, even decades, I allowed my unflappable optimism to be slowly replaced by bitterness, distrust, and pessimism. The constant bombardment of gloom and doom portrayed in the media eroded my sense of hope.

My youthful exuberance that allowed me to find the silver lining in every cloud was replaced by fatalistic negativity. "What if?" was replaced with "Why try?" The climax of my transition from positivity to hopelessness occurred when my brother, who was also my best friend, passed away unexpectedly.

There was no silver lining. There wasn't an ounce of optimism left in my body. For nearly a decade, I fell into a black hole of negativity to which there was no escape. My wife experienced my demise. My sons experienced my mental collapse. I experienced a depth of pessimism that would eventually force me to look at the man in the mirror. And I didn't like what I saw.

The first step out of the abyss of negativity was to identify all the good in my life. My family. My job. My home. Nature. My faith. Slowly, I saw a silver lining again. The change in perspective, while admittedly slow and arduous, was also encouraging and became the impetus for Fresh A.I.R.

Eliminating negativity is often like breathing with asthma: It can be labored and painful. After all, we are surrounded by negativity. Nearly every news item or movie focuses on the worst aspects of human existence. Murders, robberies, wars, disease, natural disasters…humans are driven to stare at the proverbial train wreck.

Instead of allowing all the negativity to fill our days, we should consider limiting our exposure to social media and the news. Rather, we should consider reading a book, playing board games with the family, hiking in nature, or better still, engaging in acts of service for others who are less fortunate. After all, when was the last time you helped someone in need and felt miserable after you helped them?

Unfortunately, for the past several years, society has become dishearteningly and exponentially more divided, and this negativity has spread to all aspects of life. Society is quickly losing its optimism, but it doesn't need to wait until it entirely loses hope before it changes course.

There's nothing quite like taking a deep breath of Fresh A.I.R. to clear our minds and eliminating negativity in our lives.

The Fourth Breath: *Avoid* Bandwagons

Hopping on bandwagons eliminates our individuality and our ability to think critically. Bandwagons are one of the most common fallacies, and they usually stunt our intellectual growth. Doing something just because everyone else is doing it does not make one more intelligent or better than someone else.

People are social creatures, and as such, they have a need for acceptance. Unfortunately, however, they often seek acceptance without considering accountability, integrity, or respect before they act. The need for acceptance is not a new concept. In fact, marketing companies take advantage of society's tendency to want to be part of the "in" crowd.

Nearly every commercial or advertisement focuses less on the quality of the product or service being sold and more on how this product will increase a person's social status. Yet few people care to analyze or research the product they are buying. The majority of people would rather pay more to be popular than to actually purchase a quality product or service. Image is everything, so they jump on every bandwagon that will enhance how others view them.

Think about any product that is endorsed by a celebrity. Are we buying the product for its quality, or are we buying it because a celebrity told us to do so? If it weren't for bandwagon mentality, celebrities would not be needed to sell products. Athletes and celebrities have no clue about manufacturing quality products. They get paid to use their likeness, and the products they endorse cost much more simply to pay for the celebrities' endorsements.

Bandwagons are egocentric by their very nature. When we are entirely focused on our personal images and how others see us, we often lose the ability to breathe Fresh A.I.R.

As a youth, I remember being repeatedly admonished about bandwagon mentality. "If your friends jumped off a cliff, would you follow them?"

Yet society is often manipulated to follow the crowd without taking the time to think about the consequences of its choices. At the beginning of Fresh A.I.R. the challenge was made to "start with the man (or woman) in the mirror." Unfortunately, if we are riding the bandwagon, too many reflections will show in our looking glass, and we may never see the one person we should be seeking to change.

The next time a fad or trend takes hold, whether locally or nationally, before jumping on the bandwagon, take a step back, and listen to the sage advice of Albert Einstein: "What is right is not always popular and what is popular is not always right."

When we take our own breaths without jumping on the bandwagon and inhaling the carbon dioxide of others' breaths, the A.I.R. is the Freshest.

The Fifth Breath: *Turn from Hate*

Since 2008, this country has become increasingly divided. Barely a day passes without opposing viewpoints causing riots and violence. Hateful vitriol is freely spewed whenever someone disagrees. Stereotypes have now become the norm instead of the logical fallacy they once were.

Everyone is lumped together in two opposing baskets: on one side, everyone is deplorable, a conservative, a racist, a jingoist, a bigot, a religious nut case, and an uneducated hick. In the other basket, everyone is a woke liberal, a tyrannical socialist, a hypocrite, a drug addict, or anti-American.

Fresh A.I.R. challenges you to stop breathing the pollution the government and media are spewing. Let's turn from hate to find common ground with our neighbors on an individual basis. And just because we may disagree doesn't automatically make either side inherently evil.

Hate is the antithesis to Fresh A.I.R. Instead of dwelling negatively on the fact we are different, let's embrace the unifying qualities that helped build this nation: love, freedom, pride in our country, hard work, serving others, compassion, and empathy. Let's respect our differences and enjoy the opportunities that come from allowing everyone to be unique. By the same token, we should avoid forcing our uniqueness on others. When others disagree, allow them the freedom to express themselves without casting insults, screaming, or threatening violence.

One way to stem the tide of hate might be to reduce our dependency on the media, including social media. The information from these sources is biased and merely increases the division within society.

In my classroom, whenever I assigned an argumentative research paper, I forced students to only use scholarly sources. They were not allowed to use the media to support their claims. They also were not allowed to use sources on the first page of Google unless the information came from a peer-reviewed scholarly source.

While my approach may be considered harsh or unfair (and students frequently expressed their displeasure in my stringent research rules), I want my students to dig deeper and search for truth outside the parameters that the media has set. Because every news media outlet is biased, whether to the left or to the right, if we rely solely on the media for our information, we will never know the truth.

Besides, the media has been complicit with our politicians in creating a great divide. Think of all the friendships that have dissolved in the past twenty years due to political differences, conflicting viewpoints, or cultural differences.

Unfortunately, hatred is fickle and frequently changes its targets. Shortly after September 11, 2001, this country was united in a way not seen since World War II. The bombing of the World Trade Center made us forget our differences. Heck, even Red Sox fans were pulling for the Yankees to win the World Series that year.

But while we were united in empathy, compassion, and pride in our country, we also allowed politicians and the media to stir up hatred, not just for one country, but an entire region. Much like the Japanese Americans in WWII, Americans of Middle Eastern descent became the targets of suspicion, disrespect, and violence. The media helped fuel the negative stereotyping with their narratives. Politicians constantly reminded us who the perpetrators were. While it was true that many Middle Easterners do not like the United States and would like to see its demise, it does not suggest all Middle Easterners hold those beliefs.

Twelve years later, when the Boston Marathon was bombed, old wounds were reopened, and the fires of hatred of Middle Easterners were rekindled. The media was quick to fan those flames of hatred and instead of focusing on the individuals who carried out the heinous bombing, they once again focused on an entire culture and religion. And the politicians were quick to piggyback off the narrative.

Now, over ten years later, politicians and the media seek new enemies to divide the country and spread hate. In the absence of foreign attacks on our country, they now target ethical, moral, and biological ideologies instead of specific cultures or people. But we must not let them succeed in dividing the country. We must turn from hate.

Only by turning from hate can we truly enjoy a breath of Fresh A.I.R.

The Sixth Breath: *H*elp Those in Need

While I worked at a previous employer, Human Resources sent emails requesting sick time donations for employees who had medical emergencies and needed to take time off from work for treatment but did not have any vacation or sick days left. Employees were allowed to accrue unlimited sick days, and I rarely take any days off from work, so I had amassed over two hundred hours of sick time. One particular request caught my attention because it wasn't the employee who was sick, but her child was extremely ill. They needed to travel for the treatment and would be gone for over a week.

When Human Resources reached out to find volunteers to donate their sick time, I offered to give up an entire week of my sick time to assist the employee. HR stated there was a two-day maximum per volunteer, per occurrence, so I donated two sick days. The best part of this was knowing I had done so anonymously, and the employee would never know who the donors were.

Several years ago, as I was leaving the grocery store one evening, I noticed a Ford pickup truck with its hood open. I asked the stranger what the problem was, and he stated that his starter had been giving him problems for a while. He had just picked up a new starter and stopped at the grocery on the way home to pick up dinner for his family. He was going to change the starter the next day at his friend's house, but unfortunately, the starter had completely died, and he didn't have any tools with him.

I usually keep tools in my truck, but on this day, I drove my wife's car to the store. I told the stranger, "Hey, I only live two miles away. Let me run home and get my truck, and I'll replace it for you." Flabbergasted by my offer, he managed a humble "Thanks. That would be awesome." I made the short drive home and swapped vehicles.

When I got back to the grocery store, the stranger was sitting in his truck. I parked a few spots away, grabbed my toolbox, and walked to the stranger's truck.

He looked up and saw me, and in obvious disbelief, he sheepishly uttered, "I can't believe you came back."

"No worries…I really do live that close." I took out my ratchet and sockets, and in ten minutes, I replaced the starter. Older Ford starters are held in place by three bolts and the positive battery cable, so it was an easy fix.

"Fire it up!" I blurted confidently. The stranger turned the key, and the truck started.

"Thank you" was all he could manage. I could tell by his humble countenance that he truly appreciated my help.

"You bet. Have a good night."

Look around. It is not difficult to find someone who needs a hand. Simple acts of service don't have to cost a dime but might be invaluable to the recipient. Shovel a driveway without being asked. Hold a door for someone who has their hands full. You'd be surprised how much a simple "Thank you" may impact someone's day. Or how about a smile? Yes, a smile can help someone in need of something positive in their day.

Besides, when was the last time you helped anyone who was truly in need and regretted it?

The A.I.R. we breathe is often the Freshest when we help others.

The Seventh Breath: *E*ncourage Others (and Yourself)

In the early to mid-1990s, *Saturday Night Live* actor Al Franken performed skits as Stuart Smalley, a self-help guru whose "daily affirmations" inspired people to believe in themselves. He encouraged people to look in the mirror and repeat the words, "I'm good enough, I'm smart enough, and doggone it, people like me." While mostly ironic and over the top, there is some truth as to the influence of positivity in one's life.

Even the most optimistic person needs an occasional mental boost. When the opportunity presents itself to offer support or hope to someone, are we in tune with their needs? Oftentimes, we are so wrapped up in our own world that we may miss the cues others may subtly convey.

Several years ago, a prospective student approached me. She was returning to school after a decade, and she wanted to know the best path for her. As Academic Support coordinator, I frequently had students come to me for advice about their future.

This particular student was returning but had not yet chosen a degree program or career path. The more we talked, the more it became apparent that she was an artist but had been convinced art was not a "real degree." When she showed me examples of her work, I immediately knew she needed to be an art major. That was her passion.

But when I suggested art as her degree, she caught me off guard with her response, "My family and boyfriend told me not to waste my time with art and get a real degree. Besides, I'm not good enough."

One of the most frustrating aspects of being an educator is when talented students are discouraged from chasing their dreams, especially when family and friends are the offenders. This prospective student had talent, and I was not going to allow it to be wasted.

I encouraged her to place one of her works in the upcoming art exhibit in the campus student union building. Students would be judging the art, and there would be prizes, including scholarships.

Reluctantly, she agreed. I told her I would search for her work, so she needed to promise that she would enter something into the exhibit. A few weeks later, I kept my promise and searched for her entry. I couldn't hide my smile when I saw her name on one of the exhibits. The students' votes would be counted at the end of the week, and results would be announced the following Monday.

When Monday arrived, I was quietly working in my office when the student rushed into my office and gleefully screeched, "I won!"

My response wasn't the most articulate: "Now do you believe you are good enough?!" The "I told you so" approach was all I could muster in the moment. She had caught me unprepared, and my personal joy overcame any sense of eloquence.

She thanked me again, gave me a hug, left my office, walked down the hall to admissions, and applied for the next semester…as an art major.

We all have rough patches in our lives where we feel the whole world is against us, including those closest to us. But what a tremendous boost it gives us when someone offers words of encouragement. These uplifting words can change our perspective and help us overcome a seemingly insurmountable trial or obstacle.

The next time you see or hear someone who may be struggling, stop and offer encouragement. Sometimes, words of encouragement may not be enough, and we may need to physically help. But any help, especially when unsolicited, may give the recipient the motivation to persevere and eventually succeed.

And while you are encouraging others, don't forget to channel your inner Stuart Smalley and give yourself some words of encouragement.

Now that your mind is clear, enjoy the Fresh A.I.R.!

APPENDIX A
Tenet 2

Words to which you took offense	What sparked the offense?	How you responded to the offense	How you could avoid taking offense next time

Who was told "no"?	Their reaction to being told "no"	How they responded to the offense	How they could avoid taking offense next time